"Honest and vulnerable . . . will be reassuring to many who are reaching out for some sense of meaning to shattering life changes."
—Michael Cecil, Co-founder, The Ashland Institute

"A delightful invitation to a very different experience of a fearsome diagnosis. The author proves how facing a cancer diagnosis with courage, love, and never-ending openness, gives immeasurable richness to the journey."
—Joelle Schumacher

"The book is not only inspirational; I could actually 'feel' what the author went through—his pain, confusion, and resolution."
—Risa McFarland, Montessori M.T., Community Child Advocate

"An eye-opening and heart-opening gift to anyone struggling with a cancer diagnosis. Wrapped in Christopher Foster's expert and loving embrace, you'll be inspired to meet your inevitable fears and amazingly discover that they don't have to consume you. We can all learn from Christopher's experience with cancer. It is a testament to the resilience of the human spirit and a potent invitation to realize the power of love that lies at the heart of each precious moment."
—Gail Brenner, Ph.D., Author, *The End of Self-Help: Discovering Peace and Happiness Right at the Heart of Your Messy, Scary, Brilliant Life.*

"Full of wisdom expressed with humility and openness. It is more than accurate . . . it is the truth. This book will join several others that I keep, securely, and revisit periodically."

—Mark Schmidt, computer manufacturing engineer (Rtd)

"The author shows a wonderful spirit and sense of humor about a terrifying disease. I complete agree with his quote from the survivor named Denise that once you have had cancer you are never the same again. I also believe that everything happens for a reason, all you have to do is to listen and wait and you will eventually learn what it is."

—Lenda Schwarz

"I recently lost a dear friend to cancer. In the midst of her pain and frustrations, I saw tremendous peace and love emanating from her. This book helps me see where this love comes from."

—Robin Roberts

"Inspirational and totally worthwhile if it helps just one person go out and get their colonoscopy."

—Steve Workman, workmandesign.com.

THE UPSIDE OF CANCER

HOW A TERRIFYING ILLNESS CAN LEAD YOU TO A NEW LIFE

CHRISTOPHER FOSTER

Singing Spirit Books
Denver, Colorado

Singing Spirit Books
singingspiritbooks.com

Editor: Melissa Wuske, melissaannewuske.com
Cover design: Kathi Dunn, dunn-design.com
Interior design: Dorie McClelland, springbookdesign.com

ISBN: 978-0-9711796-3-9

Revised Edition

This book is dedicated to my wife, JoAnn,
the doctors and nurses at
Kaiser Permanente Colorado,
and everyone whose life
has been touched by cancer.

CONTENTS

INTRODUCTION:

SEEING CANCER (AND LIFE) IN A NEW LIGHT

You gain strength, courage, and confidence
by every experience in which
you really stop to look fear in the face.
—Eleanor Roosevelt

There's no history of cancer in my family, and it was a shock, to put it mildly, when I was diagnosed with colon cancer in the fall of 2013.

But here's the surprising thing: despite the fear and discomfort I experienced following my diagnosis, I am happier now than I have ever been.

It is as if the cancer—designated stage 2—has forced me to go deeper into the courage and wisdom of my true nature. I've discovered, in the process, that our true nature is not fear—it is love, which as the disciple John proclaimed, "casts out all fear."

Don't get me wrong. Fear still arises. But as I move forward in my 80s I find that almost anything makes me happy now: watching a bird, saying hello to a server in my favorite coffee shop, listening to the sounds of a nearby creek, washing the dishes.

My new happiness has a boundless quality to it. I am dreaming new dreams and setting new goals even though at the same time I am becoming more practical in various ways. This is extraordinary, because I have always been a poet and a dreamer at heart; my wife, JoAnn, is the practical one.

For example, I used to be quite casual about money. I only had time for what I thought of as "spiritual" concerns and aspirations. But now I see money with new eyes: I respect it and appreciate it. I used to look down my nose at tools too—just like my Dad—but now I actually enjoy doing simple maintenance around our house. JoAnn is so impressed she says I'm a new person. "Who's there?" she calls out sometimes when I come home from the coffee shop and she hears the kitchen door open. "New person," I reply. How I love her hearty response: "That's right."

I share this brief report about my experience with cancer thus far because you too may have been diagnosed with this terrifying illness; and if this is so, I would like to share these heartfelt words with you:

First of all, please take this new adventure one step at a time. My wife has been drilling this simple wisdom into me for years, and it really is the only way to handle the challenges life brings to us.

I can only speak from my own experience. But what I have discovered, and continue to discover is that there are two ways we can look at this phenomenon we call cancer.

We can see it as the grievous and terrifying event which it obviously is. But we can also see cancer as a catalyst that can help us face our fear—especially the fear of death—and awaken to the presence of that which is not dismayed by any calamity: the inner peace at the core of our being.

I salute you in your time of trial. May this little book remind you of the courage, wisdom and profound peace of your true nature just waiting to emerge in greater fullness.

My heart is with you. Blessings to you.

1

COURAGE

*"Courage is the most important of all the virtues
because without courage,
you can't practice any other virtue consistently."*

—Maya Angelou

My life changed in an instant when Dr. Piasecki, one of my doctors at Kaiser Permanente called me on a pleasant fall afternoon. She was calm and professional, but I could feel the concern in her voice as she told me a biopsy she had taken following a routine colonoscopy showed I had colon cancer.

I listened with a mix of bewilderment and disbelief as she said she had referred me to Dr. Brown, a good surgeon she had worked with for many years, for an initial consultation.

The call was like a bolt of lightning out of a clear blue sky. I mean, how could this be? Haven't I been a seeker of truth all my life? It's true that I'm not especially religious, but I am spiritual.

As a child of 15, I cried out suddenly to my father one day at the lunch table in our middle-class home in South London, "I want to find the truth of life."

It didn't go over very well. My dad, a veteran reporter who got his first job on a London daily newspaper when he was only 19 years old, was horrified—perhaps understandably so. We began to argue. "There's no such thing as truth," he shouted at one point as our exchange became more and more heated. I will never forget the dismay on my mother's face as dad slapped me across the face, and without a word, churning with anger I stood and left the room.

Now, decades later, the doctor's news left me wondering: haven't I done my best to be true to myself and listen to my inner voice no matter where it took me? I'm active. I love life. I love my wife. I love nature. I try to stay fit. I go for a walk every day and lift weights three times a week. Not only that, I'm in my 80s, for goodness sake. I've had more than enough drama and tragedy in my life already, thank you very much.

But cancer found me out. And though I didn't know it at the time, as uncertainty, dismay and fear rose up in me, cancer would become my mentor.

We have all had many teachers, many mentors through the course of our lives. When I was a young fellow looking for meaning in an alien world, I carried Walt Whitman's *Leaves of Grass* with me in my coat pocket for two years. Wherever I went, Walt went too.

But cancer can be a teacher too. The root of the word "education" is the Latin "educo," to draw forth. Cancer, as I've mentioned, has the power to draw forth from us qualities of our true nature essential to a courageous, happy, meaningful life.

Before Dr. Piasecki even finished her call—before I

had even begun to digest what she was saying—I knew at a primeval level that it would take all the courage I had and then some to handle this challenge. Aristotle, that wise man, had it right. "Courage is the first of human qualities," he declared, "because it is the quality that guarantees all the others."

Patience and Stubbornness

It takes patience and stubbornness to be a writer. It takes patience and stubbornness to get old. And it takes patience and stubbornness to wait a month or more for a preliminary consultation with a surgeon who holds the keys to your future in his hands.

I made the best use I could of that waiting period. For example, I have always loved walking. I figured I might as well enjoy going for a walk every day while I had the chance, even though my body was showing signs of weakness and strain, not surprising given my diagnosis.

I made it a point every day to visit a favorite spot where three or four stepping-stones provide a bridge across a small creek that flows year-round at the edge of our townhome property. I love to stand on these rocks and listen to the sound of the water and watch how skillfully and effortlessly it swirls around the boulders.

I sometimes think that this Colorado stream where I like to linger has a lesson for you and me in these difficult days. If we trust life and stay in the flow of life—no matter what our age—we too will find artful ways to deal with the obstacles that appear in our lives from time to time.

As I waited as patiently as possible for my coming surgery, I found myself thinking quite a bit about mortality. My mortality. All of a sudden, it wasn't a theory any more. It really was possible that I was going to lose this physical body that had been such a loyal and faithful friend—and lose it, perhaps, quite soon.

I had thought, in all honesty, that I was more or less at peace with the notion of death. But I realized the fear of dying goes deep—and that I would need to go deep if I was going to face this ancient fear and experience the inner peace for which I had longed all my life.

MEETING MY SURGEON

Following a pre-op appointment with a nurse practitioner—who investigated, with painstaking thoroughness, if my aging body could handle the surgery that lay ahead—the day of my initial consultation with Dr. Brown arrived.

A nurse showed JoAnn and me into a large room that looked more like an operating area than a doctor's office, with a large examining table in the center of the room and lots of bright lights. As we sat in our chairs and waited to finally meet Dr. Brown—it was evident he was running late—I had a strong feeling that I would know as soon as he arrived whether I liked him and could trust him.

I have had this kind of instinct before at other important moments in my life. When Dr. Brown finally showed up, he was professional, but also unassuming and personable. I can picture him now, a big grin on his face as he reached out his hand to welcome us. He was dressed simply in slacks and an open-necked shirt—no white coat to be seen anywhere. I did indeed feel an immediate sense of connection with him. After examining me and explaining some of the details surrounding my surgery, Dr. Brown pointed out that he wouldn't really know how extensive the cancer was until he had me on the operating table.

With the help of a whiteboard, he explained that the cancer might be confined to my colon—which would be good news—or it might have begun to spread beyond the colon walls, which would be bad news and might require chemotherapy. He said it would be up to me to approve or disapprove such treatment, a remark that caught my attention. I filed it away carefully for future reference.

The surgery at a hospital north of Denver on December 26, 2013, lasted for more than three hours, and I was in the hospital for a week. Talk about patience. Talk about one step at a time. The pain wasn't too bad, thanks to the epidural device inserted into my back. But when I first woke up after the surgery, I couldn't move. I was helpless as a babe. I couldn't go to the bathroom. I couldn't feed myself.

It was a long, challenging week. But soon I was able to sit up in bed just a little. A bit later, with a friendly nurse to encourage me, I sat up on the side of the bed and actually put my feet on the floor. Patience be damned. I managed to shuffle a few feet to the bathroom under my own power, trailing the epidural and IV behind me, with the nurse holding onto me so I didn't fall.

Soon after that I took my first tentative walk around the ward, again with a nurse at my side keeping an eye on me.

Dr. Brown had to leave the hospital for a few days

after the surgery, but he appointed a member of his team to take his place. "The bed is your enemy," Dr. Brown's colleague told me the day following the surgery, and I did my best to pay heed to his advice.

It was more than an hour's drive to and from the hospital for JoAnn, but she visited me every day for seven days. What a lifesaver it was to see her face. What a lifesaver to be able to call her from the hospital when I was feeling down.

I first met JoAnn in 1995, and we married two years later. It was a marriage made in Heaven. Who would have thought that a writer and dreamer from London would meet up with a quilter and down-to-earth soul born of pioneering stock in Lawrence, Kansas?

And yet through a chain of events I won't go into here, we found each other. What can I say? It is a strange combination but it works. And without JoAnn's constant support and encouragement during the days and months following my diagnosis, my journey would have been a desolate one indeed.

We need each other in this world, don't we? What a paradox life is. We have to take personal responsibility for our own lives and yet none of us can do it alone.

A Six-Month Recovery

I was a pathetic figure when JoAnn finally brought me home from the hospital on January 2, 2014. Her daughter, Sherrie, was waiting for us with a wheelchair. I'm six feet tall and normally weigh 155 pounds, but I was down to 133 pounds as I clawed my way out of the car and deposited myself thankfully in the wheelchair.

God, it was good to be home. But while I had survived one challenge, another loomed. Dr. Brown had warned me that it generally takes six months to fully recover from my procedure, and I worried whether I would be able to walk properly after I returned home.

I love walking—I was born in Britain, after all, and I've been a walker all my life. Shuffling around a ward was one thing; but would I be able to go for proper hikes again on my favorite trails?

Fortunately, Kaiser sent a physiotherapist to our home to help me begin walking again. His name was Mike and he was a young, no-nonsense guy who got to work immediately. I could barely totter from one room to another, using rails and walls for support. But what did Mike do? As soon as he had introduced himself, he asked me to walk in a straight line down our hallway, placing one foot directly in front of the other foot to help me get my balance back. He also advised me to stand as upright as possible so as not to develop a hump in my back.

It seemed like a tall order to me, but he was on hand to help if necessary, so I gave it my best shot. Mike seemed reasonably pleased. But then he asked me to do the same thing in reverse. What? Are you kidding? I've been home for two days and this is what he wants me to do? JoAnn told me later that her heart ached for me as I struggled valiantly to follow his instructions, placing one foot behind me at a time and trying my best to keep in a straight line.

Two or three days later Mike had another bright idea. "Let's go for a walk outside," he said as soon as he entered the house. Huh? I thought. Outside? Can't we rest and chat a bit first?

It was the first time I had ventured outside without a wheelchair to sit in, but with Mike holding my arm, I navigated my way down the steps from our porch to the sidewalk that connects the various units of our town-home complex together. Then the two of us, like some kind of odd couple, began to walk slowly and laboriously to the end of our block. I was feeling quite proud of myself, but then Mike had another brilliant idea.

"Let's walk up the hill," he said. The street that leads out of our neighborhood has quite a steep slope to it. This was getting serious. Walk up the hill? Was he crazy? I couldn't do that. But I drew myself together and, at roughly the speed of a snail, we advanced together part way up the hill.

Mike's schedule allowed him to make five visits, after which I was on my own. I am truly grateful for his help. He helped me get started with my recovery, but now it was up to me. Taking a cue from Mike's sometimes outlandish assignments, I had a brilliant idea. The sidewalk that runs past our front door makes a loop around two blocks of townhomes and then passes by our front door again.

"I wonder if I could walk around the loop under my own steam?" I asked myself. I put on my walking shoes, plucked up my courage, and set out on my next adventure. It worked. One step at a time. I walked around two blocks and arrived back at our front door feeling very pleased with myself.

JoAnn was in her room quilting, but I yelled out to her and boasted how well I had done. "Well done, Papa Bear," she called back. She calls me Papa Bear and I call her Momma Bear.

Another wild idea entered my mind. "Hmm. I wonder if I could do that once more?" I thought. So I did one more circuit, walking on the grass some of the time as Mike had suggested because you have to work harder to keep your balance that way and it helps you rehabilitate sooner. One step at a time: the only way to cope with the vicissitudes life throws at us.

FINDING THE COURAGE TO FACE AN ONCOLOGIST

I was rather dreading my first meeting with Dr. Heather Hue, my oncologist.

It was nothing personal. The very word "oncologist" was enough to send tremors up my spine. I had handled my initial diagnosis. I had survived the surgery. I had begun a long and difficult recovery. But I had never met an oncologist. What would she look like? Would I feel a sense of trust in her? What was she going to say? Would she recommend some drastic treatment for me?

I was nervous, I admit, as a nurse showed JoAnn and me into Dr. Hue's office.

She was running late. Ten minutes went by. Half-an-hour went by. Impatience got the better of me and finally I decided to step into the corridor and have a little look-around.

But then, almost immediately, as I was staring up and down the corridor I saw a young woman racing down the hallway toward me with a big smile on her face. Octogenarians appreciate good-looking women like any other men. Dr. Hue, that morning, was wearing an elegant Southwestern style outfit with high black boots and a beautiful necklace, and, as she invited me into her office, I came face to face with a dream oncologist.

The impatience I had been feeling about the long wait quickly melted away as we began to talk. Dr. Hue has a strong, comforting presence, and the more we spoke, the more at peace I felt and the more I knew I was in good hands. She was raised in Los Alamos, she told us, where her dad was a physicist and her mom was a school teacher. She said she would have me under active surveillance for five years.

"Let me do the worrying," Dr. Hue declared, as she explained the various stages of cancer and how I was stage 2. She said that if I were younger she would probably recommend chemotherapy, but because of my age she did not recommend going that route.

I walked out of her office with my courage renewed. I knew I had found a strong, kind, capable ally to help me on my journey into the unknown.

2

WISDOM

"Wisdom begins in wonder."
—Socrates

When I think about cancer and the challenge it brings, I am thankful for a profound lesson life has taught me over the years: wisdom is always present with us but we must be still if we want to hear its quiet voice speaking to us in our heart.

I first learned this lesson during a difficult time in my life when I returned home to London as a young man to "settle down" after spending nearly three years working as a reporter in Southern Rhodesia—now Zimbabwe—and roaming around New Zealand and Australia.

I was 22, an only child, and for a while it felt good to be home. But I soon began to feel alienated from my job as a reporter on the *Daily Express* and indeed from my entire middle-class British existence. An inner voice kept saying there was more to life than I was experiencing.

I had a nice girlfriend named Susan. I had a small sailing boat, which I kept at Maldon, on the Essex coast, and sailed with a passion. There was a good career ahead of me, potentially. And yet I felt lost and alone in an alien world.

What was I to do with this strange discontent brewing within me? And then one day, as if out of nowhere, a strange, exhilarating idea entered my mind.

"I could go to British Columbia," I thought to myself, "where there is freedom and space and I will surely find the meaning and truth for which I long."

I realized that just because my dad was a reporter all his life, living what seemed to me at the time a rather limited British middle-class existence, didn't mean that I had to follow in his footsteps.

I didn't know a soul in Canada, but that didn't seem to matter. It was as if an inner voice—a strong, irresistible inner voice—was showing me a path whereby I might fulfill my destiny.

The more I thought about this strange idea that had erupted in my mind, the more excited I became: yet I could not help but feel conflicted at the thought of leaving my family and girl-friend and giving up a promising career with the *Daily Express*.

What was the right thing to do? As I thrashed the idea around in my mind, my inner voice spoke again: "Find a quiet place by the sea where you can be still and commune with nature and you will know what to do." And that was exactly how it worked out.

I took a train to the Sussex coast and walked along the beautiful cliffs called the Downs. It was May and the sea was a brilliant blue. I stopped to listen to the skylarks filling the air with their song, and I knew in that instant—with every fiber of my being—that it was the right thing for me to go to British Columbia.

LISTENING TO OUR INNER WISDOM

Since that long-ago experience I have learned that wisdom is always speaking to me in the quietness of my heart, just as it is always speaking to you—we just have to be still and listen.

Thus when cancer found me out and I faced perhaps the biggest challenge of my life—not knowing, really, whether I would live or die—I made it a habit to seek stillness, especially when fear was knocking at my door and especially in the early morning and evening.

"I'm going to meditate," I would tell my wife so that she knew I wanted to be quiet.

I'm not talking about a formal meditation practice. I simply sat down and surrendered. I surrendered to the reality of my diagnosis. I surrendered to the possibility of losing my physical form. And I surrendered, above all, to the quietness of eternal being that is present with each of us as long as we live.

I kept a notebook beside me as I meditated, so that I could write down some of my thoughts and realizations.

I also did some abdominal breathing, which I find very relaxing, counting my breath each time I sucked air into my belly and—when my mind wandered—going back to the beginning and starting again.

JOY IN THE MIDST OF FEAR

I made a remarkable discovery as I deliberately sought refuge in stillness in the face of the fear that ebbed and flowed within me following my diagnosis.

What I had thought was fear transformed in an instant into pure, radiant joy as a door opened in my heart and I became conscious of the presence of the divine.

There is an antidote to fear. All we have to do is to be still, and look for the faint feeling of God's eternal presence—our own presence, dare I say—in the background of all other experience.

Is it possible that fear, this demon that ruins so many lives, is actually an ally that can help us become more conscious of the presence of the divine in our lives?

I realized something else, too, as I persisted with my meditations. The peace and joy I was experiencing in the midst of fear was not coming to me from some far-off place. It was my own peace. It was my own joy bubbling up within me—the joy that is the birthright of every one of us, even in the midst of cancer, especially in the midst of cancer.

We talk a lot these days about happiness, and there is nothing wrong with happiness, of course. But there is no joy like the joy that waits to blossom in you and me as we turn our attention away from fear and focus instead on the presence of eternal love.

Here are a few entries from the notebook I kept handy during my meditations:

"In Thy presence, Lord, there is no fear."

"In my presence there is no fear."

"I can overcome my fear. I not only can overcome it, but I am overcoming it as I remember my presence and turn to it."

"When I open to the presence of the eternal I don't feel on my own anymore."

"When I am not afraid of death, I am not afraid of cancer."

JoAnn and Her "Radar"

As I've mentioned, I was painfully weak when I came home from the hospital. In many ways, the six-month recovery was a bigger challenge for me than the surgery or the diagnosis. There were times when I wondered if I really would make a full recovery and live a normal, active life again.

Enter my wife and her "radar."

JoAnn is very good at being still and listening to her inner wisdom. She calls it her radar.

We sleep in separate rooms but we get together for a cuddle when we wake up. Early one morning, during a challenging period in my recovery, JoAnn came into my room for a hug with her eyes shining, radiating happiness, and said she had something important to share with me.

She told me that before going to sleep, she realized that we couldn't handle our situation by ourselves, and she called out to the universe for help.

She woke suddenly at three in the morning with a profound sense of assurance that everything was going to work out very well and I was going to come through my affliction just fine.

I have learned to trust my wife's radar implicitly. Her quiet words of assurance to me that morning meant the world to me. She has a way of accessing the wisdom of the universe—the wisdom that is our best friend and will never let us down—that is unique and beyond anything I can do.

There is a turning point in every cycle. I believe that was the moment when the tide began to turn for me and I knew in my heart that I would get well.

FOLLOWING OUR HUNCHES

Do you sometimes look back and marvel how your whole life changed because you followed a hunch— even though it perhaps seemed a bit weird or insignificant?

With hindsight, I realize that long before cancer entered my life, my inner wisdom was charting a path that would not only help me meet my challenges, but would lead me in the most helpful and beneficial direction possible—that would give me the best chance to achieve my dreams.

On July 4, 1995, I was living in a senior citizens' apartment block in Vancouver, British Columbia, devastated and demoralized by two grave losses. The spiritual community in the interior of BC that had been my home for 36 years—where among other things I edited a local weekly newspaper and wrote

several books—had collapsed following the death of
its leader in 1988; then my former wife, Joy, suffered
a fatal stroke as we were flying home to Vancouver
after celebrating our 25th wedding anniversary in the
Caribbean. Joy was rushed to hospital in a coma after
we landed. After an agonizing wait, a doctor told me
there was nothing they could do to help Joy and I must
make peace with the situation as best I could. As I sat,
numb with grief, at Joy's bedside, a miracle happened:
she opened her eyes for a moment and actually winked
at me. As I bent my head close to hers, I heard a whisper, soft as a falling feather, escape her lips: "Home."
At first I thought she wanted me to take her back to
our home in the interior, but then I realized she was
letting me know all was well: she was on her way to
that realm of light that is the true destiny of each of us.

ON THE EDGE OF A PRECIPICE

I was in a daze after the two events I've described. I felt
as if I was looking over the edge of a precipice.

My son, Durwin, lives in Vancouver, and I was most
thankful for his friendship and help in this difficult
time. But as I wandered around the beautiful city of
Vancouver, lost in a fog of despair, my inner voice

spoke to me through my pain: "There's a spiritual community in Colorado where you have some friends. Why not go there for a visit, perhaps you will find the support you need to help you in your grieving?"

I decided to do exactly what my inner voice had suggested. I booked a flight from Vancouver to Denver, but shortly before I was due to leave I remembered something that proved to be very important indeed: I remembered how a few years earlier a Denver woman had applied to attend a small writing workshop I was putting on in British Columbia. As it happened, she had to cancel, and I never did meet her. But I remembered her name. "Workman," I thought to myself. "I'm sure it was Workman. JoAnn Workman, I think."

My reporter instincts clicked in and I looked up "Workman" in the Denver white pages. There she was. JoAnn Workman. My wife-to-be—though I didn't know it at the time, of course.

"Why not give her a call?" my inner voice whispered. "Be brave. Go for it. Ask her if she would like to meet you for a coffee while you're in Colorado."

So that's what I did. JoAnn was alone in her small townhome when I called. She remembers vividly what she was doing just before the call came through: "I was sitting in my chair asking myself, 'Is this what I'm supposed to be doing with my life?'" she recalls. "Then two things happened almost simultaneously. I don't really know which came first: The phone rang—and I felt a presence sitting in the chair just across the room from me.

"It was all so surreal and unexpected that I was totally flustered when I picked up the phone."

JoAnn and I talked for a little while and agreed to meet while I was in Colorado. And thus began a relationship that, despite its challenges, has continued to grow and prosper and bring ever-increasing happiness and gratitude into our lives.

THE POWER OF LOVE

Cancer is a terrifying affliction. It is regarded by many people as our most-feared illness. But the power of love, which brought me through the loss of my former wife and helped me face the loss of the community that had been my home, will help both you and me now as we face the challenge of cancer or any other challenge.

Nothing is stronger than love. And nothing is stronger than the wisdom that is the ally of love and speaks love's word to us in the silence of our heart. Listen to love's quiet voice when fear arises. And remember the timeless words: "Perfect love casts out all fear."

There is a hand of love on your life that you can trust absolutely and that will bring you safely through any adversity as you listen to its quiet voice in your heart.

3

INNER PEACE

*"We don't realize that,
somewhere within us all,
there does exist a supreme self
who is eternally at peace."*
—Elizabeth Gilbert

So what are we to make of cancer? Is it the curse our culture thinks it is—for which, hopefully, we will find a cure one day soon? Or is cancer a catalyst that can help us break through into a deeper experience of our eternal nature—the peace of our "supreme self" as Elizabeth Gilbert describes it?

How about the possibility that cancer is both these things and that the universe of which we are an integral part quite enjoys paradoxes and in fact spins new ones into existence all the time?

This is how it is for me.

Consider this paradox, for example. I can't help but note these days that despite my best efforts my physical body isn't as quick or nimble as it once was. And yet I feel more engaged with life than ever. I am happier than I have ever been. I see the wonder of life and life's little moments more clearly.

Then there's this strange paradox around what we call death. I respect each person's view on this very personal matter. I seek merely to share my own perspective, and experience, which is this: yes, my body is going to die. I can't dispute that. But while I inhabit a physical form that is truly miraculous and makes it possible for me to think and feel and visit the coffee shop most afternoons—and which will one day return to the earth from whence it came—I'm becoming increasingly conscious that I am a spiritual being.

I love my body. I appreciate it and care for it as best I can as it proceeds through the aging process. But with each day that passes the more conscious I become of my eternal presence and the larger reality of which it is part—a reality that is forever untouched by this changing world.

I can't say I'm grateful, exactly, for cancer. But I am grateful—how could I not be?—that life, in its goodness, has been able to use this feared illness to make me more conscious of my true nature and the wonder of creation.

THE WONDER OF LIFE

I stepped out on the front porch early one morning recently to connect with the larger world and was suddenly overwhelmed by the grandeur of it all.

It was one of those clear, sunny days that Colorado is so good at, and as I looked up at the blue vault above me I realized, not for the first time, that here was my own boundless nature being reflected back to me.

A jet liner was streaking across the sky like a slim

white dagger and I reflected for a moment on another miracle: inside that sleek projectile were a hundred or two hundred or however many people each with their own dreams and their own part to play in the cosmic dance.

I saw vastness and I saw also the wonder of tiny things: the elegance of grass and fallen leaves; the proud blue spruce tree outside my study window that remains unperturbed by any of our human perplexities and is one of my best friends.

We are not the helpless, frightened creatures we sometimes imagine ourselves to be. We are Children of Light and it is a marvel to me that an affliction such as cancer can actually make us stronger and more in touch with life's wonder, just as it is a marvel that life always stands ready to lift us up and help us find our way through even the most dire challenge.

Consider the following powerful expressions—so in tune with the message I seek to share in this book—which I came across while browsing the website of the Pink Lotus Breast Center.

First, some words from a cancer survivor named Denise:

"I think cancer changes anyone who has gone through it . . . you can never feel as you once felt, about life and about death. For me . . . I was devastated and had a very hard time dealing with it all as I was going through all of it. I was also stage 3.

"I am a 2-year survivor now and I think I am a stronger person, I am always going to have that one little corner of fear that my cancer may come back someday, but I learned how to deal with that fear whenever it comes over me. I am less fearful more and more every day, and enjoy my life more and more every day!!!!"

Echoing the same strong, vibrant spirit, here are some words from another cancer survivor named Gina:

"Cancer can make you a stronger, sensitive, giving, appreciative, loving, and fearless person. You can have those 'Fear Moments' but release them and move on. Find your divine purpose and what you are going to do with your life. I never thought I would ever say this, but cancer changed me for the good. I am blessed for so many reasons and so are you . . . let's count our blessings together."

Yes. Yes indeed. Let us count our blessings together.

GIVING OUR GIFT

You and I have come into this world with a unique gift that only we can give.

I find as my own life journey continues that inner peace is not a static state of supposed perfection: it is the very source of the creativity and passion I need to give my gift and fulfill my destiny.

In recent months, for instance, dreams and goals that I have cherished all my life—such as the dream of being a successful writer—are rising up more strongly than ever demanding to be fulfilled.

I've loved writing since I wrote my first story as a child during the early days of the Blitz before being evacuated to the Devon countryside. I scribbled the story in an old notebook and, beaming with pride, showed it to my mother. The two of us lived together in an apartment block in central London. Dad was away in the army.

I was so grateful for my mother's strength in that challenging time. "It's all right, it's all right," she kept saying to me as I clung to her in terror one night as bombs fell all around us and the building swayed back and forth beneath us.

The itch to write has never left me. For my next

book, I'll probably try my hand at a follow-up to "The Upside" theme: "The Upside of Loss," for example, or "The Upside of Fear," or perhaps "The Upside of Prosperity."

Sometime, I'd also like to write about a story that riveted Britain in the 1960s, when my dad and another reporter were sentenced to prison for refusing to disclose their sources to a government tribunal investigating leaks about a British spy called Vassall.

Yet another idea lurking somewhere in my brain is the possibility of writing about some of the famous and sensational stories my father covered during his long career. Dad, who died at 95, was known as "Fireman Foster" in the British press community because in his early days he always seemed to be the first reporter on the scene of big London fires such as the Crystal Palace Fire of 1936. Later he covered sensational crimes such as the Haigh acid bath murders and the Brighton trunk murders.

GOD'S GUIDANCE

If you or I won a lottery one day, I'm sure we would waste no time claiming our reward. Yet we already possess a gift of enormous value given to us freely at our birth—the peace of our eternal nature which is always with us and which nothing can diminish or defile.

I see more clearly, as I age, how God—or shall I say life?—is always seeking to help us remember our true birthright. As William Cowper wrote long ago, "God moves in mysterious ways, His wonders to perform."

I remember, for example, the epiphany I experienced a few months after arriving in British Columbia from the UK as a young man and being hired as a reporter by the *Daily Colonist* newspaper in Victoria.

It's a lovely city, Victoria. Go see the Butchart Gardens sometime if you ever have the chance. Anyway, I had bought an ancient 22-foot sailboat—which, being a seeker of truth, I promptly named "Vision." One day, with a week's holiday up my sleeve, filled with anticipation, I cast off my moorings in the Inner Harbor and set out on my first cruise in the beautiful Gulf Islands of BC.

I had sailed in the sheltered waters of the Blackwater River on the East Coast of England but never in more open waters.

The sea was serene at first, but then swiftly everything changed. A strong wind blew up as I was navigating a narrow pass between two islands and I had to battle fierce rip-currents. There was a small inboard engine on the boat, but it wasn't very reliable, partly because I wasn't very good at giving it the maintenance it deserved.

I kept a desperate eye on the shore, using a tree as a marker and trying to decide if I was making any progress. For a while it seemed to me as if I was simply standing still.

I kept praying that my little motor wouldn't quit, and it didn't quit. It was a real trooper. Finally I emerged out of the pass into open water, and soon afterwards—not because of any clever planning on my part, mind you—I found myself at the entrance of a beautiful cove.

Trees lined the shores of the cove and I was enveloped in warm, soft evening air and stillness that was palpable. There was no other boat in sight as, with just a whisper of a breeze, I ghosted across the velvet surface of the lagoon.

The stillness was a balm that reached deep into my soul. It was as if the universe was enfolding me in love, and I knew that strange though my quest had seemed to my parents, it wasn't a mistake to listen to my heart and give up everything to go to Canada.

I felt at one with everything—the silky water over which my boat glided—the tree-lined shores of the cove—and the beautiful night sky with its billions of stars beaming upon me.

BRINGING THE FEAR OF DEATH INTO THE OPEN

It is 60 years or more since God touched me with its love that evening and reminded me that the peace for which I longed is always with me and that my quest for "truth" and a more meaningful life was not in vain.

And now, if you will allow me, I would reach out and remind you that you are not alone either as you face the challenge of cancer—and, perhaps, the possibility of your own death.

I mentioned in the last chapter how effective and helpful it can be, when fear arises, to be still, and move attention away from fear—which comes and goes—to the faint feeling of what does not come and go—our own ageless presence, our own being.

Can this be described? I don't think so. Can it be understood? I don't think so.

But it can be experienced. I'm experiencing it now in whatever measure as I write these words.

Yes, the fear of death is strong. We dread the unknown and have been conditioned to think that death is the end of everything. But the more time I spend turning in love to the stillness of being, the more I realize that there is no end to being. There is no end to our own eternal presence.

There is an end to our physical form, of course. But does the unconquerable spirit at the core of your being have an end? I don't think so. It is the same age now that it was when you were born, or a thousand years before that, or a thousand years hence.

We have a remarkable opportunity, you and I. With a little help from cancer perhaps, we can see death in a new light not as an end but as a journey to a more glorious experience of truth, freedom and joy.

VOYAGE INTO FREEDOM

I sometimes remember a magical evening long ago when I boarded a ship named the Homeric in South-ampton, England to sail to Canada.

It was one o'clock in the morning and the ship was due to depart at 1:30. I could feel the engines throb-bing beneath my feet as I checked out my cabin and proceeded hastily to a lounge on the upper deck. I didn't want to miss the moment when the Homeric cast off its ties to England and began its voyage.

As I sipped a cup of coffee in the lounge and looked at the lights of the harbor, the propellers began to churn, and slowly, almost imperceptibly, the great ship began to move. I was overwhelmed with a sense of freedom as it gradually picked up speed on its way to the open sea. I had no idea what lay ahead, but I was filled with joy as I faced the immense possibilities of the unknown.

This is how I see death: as a journey to a new and more glorious experience of ourselves and of freedom.

PEACE BE WITH YOU

There are three major cancer-related fears, according to The National Coalition for Cancer Survivorship, citing research literature: fear of death, fear of recurrence and fear of stigma, which is fear of being thought about or treated differently.

Yes, fear is part of human nature. But it is not part of our true nature. Fear burdens every soul on the planet and is the cause of all the world's turmoil and pain, and yet the words of the disciple John are forever true: "Perfect love casts out all fear."

As you listen to your inner wisdom and express the love that is yours to give, the happier you will become and the more at peace you will be regardless of what is happening or not happening in your life.

I leave you with some other immortal words from Psalm 46:10: "Be still, and know that I am God." I love this quote. Surely, it refers to God's living presence in each of us and has nothing to do with some far-off deity separate from ourselves.

Thank you for reading these words. My love is with you. May you experience the courage, wisdom and peace of your true nature ever more fully and abundantly.

A Note from the Author

If you enjoyed this book please consider submitting a review to Amazon. It would be a huge help to me. Just go to the following: The Upside of Cancer.

I would love to hear from you. Please email christopherfoster@comcast.net and share your own experiences, feedback or ideas with me.

Finally, please don't hesitate to recommend my book to friends or bring it to the attention of someone you think might be interested in helping spread my message. For more from me, visit my blog at http://www.thehappyseeker.com.

Other Books by Christopher Foster

Do you worry sometimes about growing older? My book, *The Secret Promise of Aging*, offers an exciting new way of thinking about this journey we all face.

Best-selling author Sharon Salzberg praises the book as "full of generous insight and truth-telling . . . will be welcomed by readers of every age."

"A bright and insightful book, and actually useful for any age," declares Ken Wilber.

With insights and stories from my own personal experience, *The Secret Promise of Aging* offers 41 practical suggestions and strategies to help you experience more of the wonder and joy that is your birthright regardless of age.

I'm also the author of *The Raven Who Spoke with God*, a classic story about following our dream and finding our passion that has been published in 11 foreign-language editions.

The Secret Promise of Aging is available in print and Kindle editions at Amazon. *The Raven Who Spoke with God* is available in a Kindle edition at Amazon.

About the Author

Christopher Foster wrote his first story as a 7-year-old living with his Mum in London amid fires and bombs in the early days of the blitz; he was later evacuated to the Devon countryside. Writing became a lifelong passion along with an even deeper longing—which he announced proudly to his Dad when he was 15 years old—to find the true meaning of life.

There was a bit of a row at the lunch table when he made his pronouncement. His father, a respected British journalist, didn't know what to make of it, and who could blame him? Chris was pretty confused himself. But he knew he didn't fit in with the traditional middle-class British environment into which he had been born. There was more to life than this—he was sure of it.

It can be a tough teacher, the seed of truth that abides in each of us wanting to be fulfilled and given greater expression. There were many lessons to learn and unlearn in various countries round the world—from Southern Rhodesia to Australia, from British Columbia to Denver, Colorado—and of course those lessons continue to this day. Christopher's cancer diagnosis in 2013 has helped him see more clearly one of life's most interesting paradoxes: fear and suffering can actually help us grow and find new happiness.

Now in his 80s, Christopher is a former reporter and weekly newspaper editor and author of six books. He lives in Denver, Colorado, and has a son and three grandchildren in British Columbia. Contact Chris at www.thehappyseeker.com or at christopherfoster@comcast.net.

Made in United States
Troutdale, OR
12/26/2024